Snakes

This is a snake.

These are snakes, too.

Some snakes are big. This snake is as big as a man.

Some snakes are little. This snake is as little as a crayon.

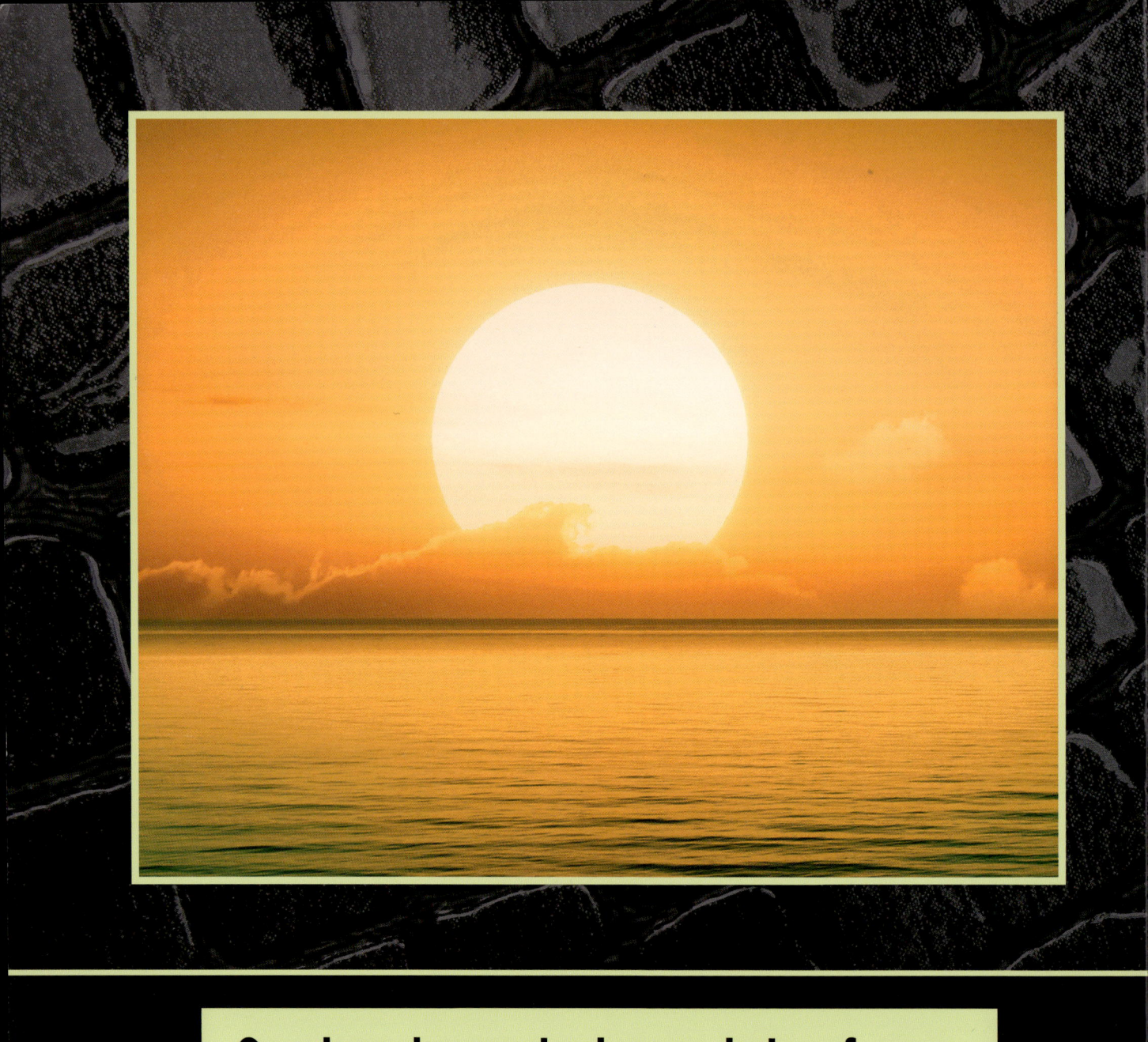

Snakes have to have lots of sun.
The sun makes them warm.

Snakes live where there is lots of sun. They can live here or here.

Snakes can't live where it is cold.
Snakes do not live here.

Snakes have to eat.

All snakes eat animals.

Many snakes eat these animals.

Some snakes eat these animals.

All snakes have scales.

All snakes make new scales.

The old scales come off.

The new scales are under the old scales.

Many snakes' scales look like where they live.

Scales can help snakes hide. Snakes hide so they can get animals to eat.

This snake is brown. It looks like the dirt. The lizard can't see it.

This snake is yellow. It looks like the leaves. The mouse couldn't see it.

This snake is brown. It looks like the trees. The squirrel couldn't see it.

Snakes have to hide from animals that want to eat them, too. All of these animals eat snakes.

This snake has red scales. The red scales can't help the snake hide.

23

The red says, "Look out! I am bad to eat!" When animals see the red scales, they will not eat this snake.

These are snake eggs. Many snakes have eggs.

This is a nest. Some snakes will lay eggs in a nest.

Baby snakes will come out of the eggs.

Some snakes don't lay eggs. See this baby snake come out of its mom.

Snakes can be big or little. Some have eggs and some don't.

All snakes have scales. All snakes eat animals. All snakes have to have the sun to live.

Snake Food Web

This is how energy flows

- Hawk
- Bullfrog
- Snake
- Mouse
- Plants
- Squirrel

31

Power Words

a	come	in	of	these
all	couldn't	is	off	they
am	do	it	or	this
animals	doesn't	its	out	to
are	don't	like	red	too
as	eat	little	see	under
baby	from	live	so	want
be	get	look	some	where
big	has	make	that	will
brown	have	many	the	yellow
can	here	new	them	
can't	I	not	there	